D0532031

CALCIUM

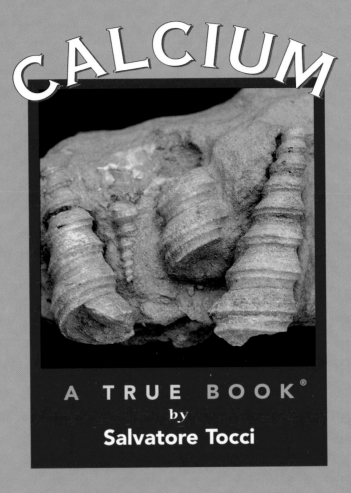

A TRUE BOOK®

by

Salvatore Tocci

Children's Press®
A Division of Scholastic Inc.

New York Toronto London Auckland Sydney
Mexico City New Delhi Hong Kong

Limestone, which contains calcium, was used to build the Empire State Building.

Reading Consultant
Julia McKenzie Munemo, EdM
New York, New York

Science Consultant
John A. Benner
Austin, Texas

The photo on the cover shows an oyster with a pearl. The photo on the title page shows fossils in limestone.

The author and the publisher are not responsible for injuries or accidents that occur during or from any experiments. Experiments should be conducted in the presence of or with the help of an adult. Any instructions of the experiments that require the use of sharp, hot, or other unsafe items should be conducted by or with the help of an adult.

Library of Congress Cataloging-in-Publication Data

Tocci, Salvatore.
    Calcium / by Salvatore Tocci.
        p. cm. — (A true book)
    Includes index.
    Contents: What do you use batteries for?—What is calcium?—How is calcium useful?—When is calcium a problem?—Why do our bodies need calcium?—Fun facts about calcium.
    ISBN 0-516-24405-1 (lib. bdg.)   0-516-27847-9 (pbk.)
    1. Calcium—Juvenile literature. [1. Calcium.] I. Title. II. Series.
QD181.C2T63 2004
546'.393—dc22
                                      2003016210

1 2 3 4 5 6 7 8 9 10 R 13 12 11 10 09 08 07 06 05 04

Contents

What Do You Use Batteries For?

How many items in your home are powered by batteries? You may use batteries to power a remote control, a clock, a flashlight, or a radio. No matter what you use them for, these batteries are small enough to hold in your hand.

In 1808, an English scientist named Sir Humphry Davy needed a very powerful battery to perform an experiment. The only way for him to get the battery he needed was to build it. When Davy was finished building his battery, it was almost the size of a small room. Building such a giant battery was the only way Davy could get the electrical power he needed to perform his experiment.

In 1808, Sir Humphry Davy used a giant battery to discover calcium.

Davy used his battery to pass electricity through a solid substance called lime. Lime is the substance people apply to their lawns to help the grass grow. Davy's battery supplied enough electrical power to break apart the lime into the building blocks that make it up. One of these building blocks is calcium.

What Is Calcium?

Calcium is an element. An **element** is the building block of matter. **Matter** is the stuff or material that makes up everything in the universe. This book, the chair you are sitting on, and even your body are made of matter.

There are millions of different kinds of matter. However, there are just a few more than one hundred different elements. How can so many different kinds of matter be made up of so few elements? Think about the English language. Just twenty-six letters can be arranged to make up all the words in the language. Likewise, the approximately one hundred elements can

Calcium is the fifth most abundant element
in Earth's crust, which is its outermost layer.

be arranged to make up all
the different kinds of matter
in the universe.

The name "calcium" comes from the word *calx,* which is Latin for lime. Every element has both a name and a symbol. The symbol for calcium is Ca, the first two letters in its name. Like most other elements, calcium is a metal. You may think that all metals, such as copper and gold, are hard and shiny. However, calcium is fairly soft and turns a dull, grayish color when it is exposed to the air.

Like all metals, this piece of calcium conducts electricity well.

All metals do have one thing in common, though. They are all good **conductors** of electricity.

Calcium is a very active metal. This means calcium reacts with almost anything it comes in contact with, including air and water. When a small piece of calcium is placed in water, bubbles of gas are produced and come to the surface. The gas that forms is highly explosive. For

Notice the gas bubbles that form when calcium comes into contact with water.

this reason, calcium is stored in special containers to keep it from coming into contact with water.

Calcium is rarely found as a pure metal in nature. Rather, calcium is usually found combined with other elements in **compounds**. A compound is a substance that is made from the combination of two or more different elements. Davy discovered calcium by passing electricity through lime. Lime is a compound made of two elements, calcium and oxygen. Compounds that contain calcium, such as lime, are very useful.

How Are Calcium Compounds Useful?

One place in the world where you can find a huge amount of calcium is the Great Barrier Reef. This reef stretches for more than 1,250 miles (2,000 kilometers) along the eastern coast of Australia. It is the world's largest coral reef.

17

Lying just below the surface of the water, this huge reef is home to many kinds of colorful fish and other animals.

The coral reef itself is also very colorful. The colors of the reef are created by the small, living animals known as polyps that make up one part of the reef. The other part of the reef is made from a sticky substance that these polyps create. Over time, this

If the Great Barrier Reef were located off the eastern coast of the United States, it would stretch from Maine to Florida.

The tiny polyps use their tentacles to capture food. When threatened, the polyps withdraw into their shells.

sticky substance hardens to form the rocky material that makes up a coral reef. This rocky material is a calcium compound called calcium carbonate. Calcium carbonate forms the shell that protects the tiny polyps. When threatened, the polyps retreat into their shells.

Animals known as mollusks also have shells made of calcium carbonate. These

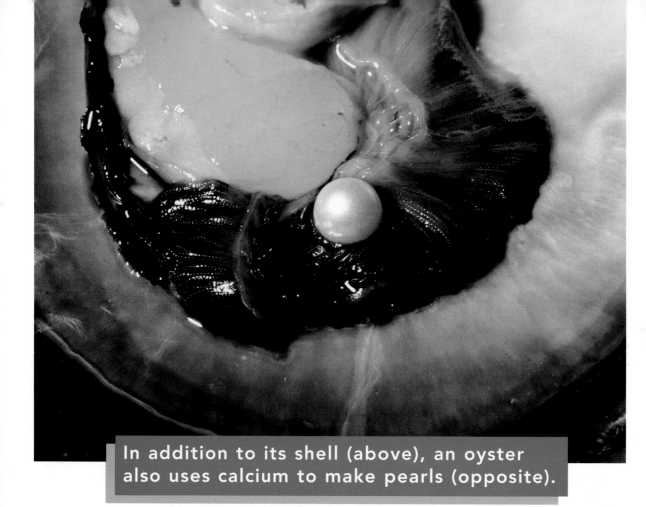

In addition to its shell (above), an oyster also uses calcium to make pearls (opposite).

animals include clams, oysters, snails, mussels, and conches. The hard shells help protect these animals from predators.

Softening Eggshells

Chickens need calcium in their feed to make the shell around their eggs. Without enough calcium, their shells would be too soft and easily broken. A chick takes about twenty-three days to hatch from an egg. If the shell breaks too soon, the chick will not be able to develop fully.

Place an egg in a glass and cover it with vinegar. The next day, pour off the vinegar. Feel the egg. The vinegar broke apart the calcium carbonate that made up the shell. As a result, the shell is soft and easily breaks.

When mollusks die, they sink to the bottom of the sea. Their soft body parts decompose, or break down, but their hard shells remain and begin to pile up on the seafloor. Slowly, the pile gets thicker and thicker, building up to hundreds of feet. The top of the pile starts to squash down, or put pressure on, the shells near the bottom. Over tens of millions of years, this pressure changes the shells into a type of rock

The walls of the Grand Canyon include limestone layers.

called **limestone**. This limestone may eventually wind up near or on Earth's surface.

Pressure and heat may change limestone that remains inside

The Jefferson Memorial is one of many buildings in Washington, D.C., that is built of marble.

Earth into **marble**. Limestone and marble are used to build buildings and create statues. The limestone and marble used by builders and sculptors may be 250 to 300 million years old.

When Is Calcium a Problem?

Compounds that contain calcium have a number of uses, from making snail shells to providing materials for statues. However, calcium can be a problem when there is too much of it. For example, having too much calcium in

Too much calcium in the soil may be keeping these plants from growing well.

their feed can cause chickens to lay eggs with shells that feel like sandpaper. These eggs do not hatch well. If there is too much calcium in the soil, plants will not grow as well.

Too much calcium can also affect the water you wash with and drink. Water with too much calcium in it is called **hard water**. Water normally contains calcium, which is dissolved in the water. In other words, the particles of calcium are so small that you cannot see them. (Dissolving is what happens when sugar is stirred into hot coffee or tea.) However, if there is too much calcium in water, not all of it can dissolve. Some of it remains as a solid that can stick to the insides of pipes, coffee pots, and tea kettles. The calcium that sticks forms a deposit that can slowly build up and clog a pipe.

Hard water can cause a sink drain to become clogged.

Hard water also reacts with soap to form a sticky substance that can leave a dark ring around a bathtub. Because soap does not produce as many suds in hard water, a person will not get as clean when washing in water that contains too much calcium. Water softeners can be used to remove the excess calcium present in hard water.

Why Do Our Bodies Need Calcium?

Your body uses calcium to build strong and healthy bones. Bones hold you up and, along with muscles, help you walk, run, jump, and even talk. Your body gets calcium from the foods

These dairy products
are rich in calcium.

you eat. Foods that are rich in calcium include dairy products, such as milk, cheese, and yogurt.

Older people sometimes do not have enough calcium in their bodies. As a result, their bones become too soft and can break easily if the people fall. This condition is called **osteoporosis**. To avoid getting osteoporosis when they get older, people often take calcium tablets.

Breaking Bones

You can see what can happen to bones that lack calcium. Ask an adult to help you remove all the skin and meat from two chicken leg bones. Try to bend one of the bones with your fingers.

Place each bone in a separate jar. Cover one bone with water and the other bone with vinegar. Cover the jars with lids, foil, or plastic wrap. Allow the bones to soak for forty-eight hours. When the time is up, drain off the water and vinegar. Try to bend each bone with your fingers. See how easy it is to break the bone that was soaked in vinegar. The vinegar removed the calcium that was in the bone, making it weak and easy to break.

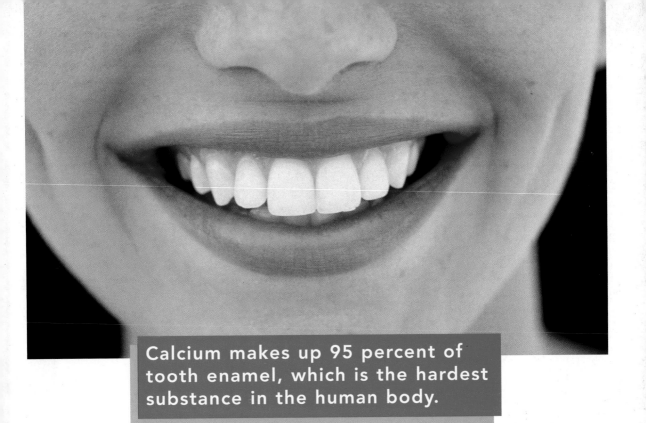

Calcium makes up 95 percent of tooth enamel, which is the hardest substance in the human body.

Calcium is also used for other jobs in the body. For example, calcium is used to make tooth **enamel**, which is the white part that you see in your mouth. The enamel covers and protects the softer parts of your teeth. Calcium is also needed for muscles to contract and for nerves to send signals through the body. Calcium also helps blood to clot when you get a cut.

Young people between the ages of nine and eighteen need the most calcium in their diets. The amount of a nutrient a person needs is called the Dietary Reference Intake (DRI). In the case of calcium,

If you eat what is shown here, you will get your recommended daily supply of calcium.

the DRI for someone between the ages of 9 and 18 is 1300 milligrams (mg) a day. Two slices of Swiss cheese, one cup of yogurt, and two glasses of whole milk supply 1,300 mg of calcium. For people between the ages of nineteen and fifty, the DRI of calcium drops to 1,000 mg a day. A person who is nineteen years old needs less calcium because by this age, all his or her bones have formed fully.

Fun Facts About Calcium

- Your bones and teeth contain more than 99 percent of the calcium in your body.

- You were born with more than three hundred bones. As you get older, these bones grow. Some of them join together, reducing the number of bones you have. By the time you turn twenty, you will have only 206 bones.

- Your body has more than six hundred muscles that depend on calcium to contract.

- Eating half of a 10-inch (25-centimeter) cheese pizza provides more calcium than drinking an 8-ounce (237-milliliter) glass of milk.

- Calcium is an ingredient in some antacid tablets that are taken to relieve upset stomachs.

- Limestone, which contains calcium, was used to build the Empire State Building, which was once the tallest building in the world.

To Find Out More

If you would like to learn more about calcium, check out these additional resources.

 **Books**

Blashfield, Jean F. **Calcium.** Austin, TX: Raintree/ Steck Vaughn, 1998.

Farndon, John. **Calcium.** NY: Benchmark Books, 2000.

McIlwain, Harris and Debra Fulghum Bruce. **Super Calcium Counter.** NY: Kensington Publishing Corp., 2000.

Pierre, Colleen. **Calcium in Your Life.** NY: John Wiley & Sons, 1997.

Organizations and Online Sites

National Osteoporosis Foundation
1232 22nd Street N.W.
Washington, D.C.
20037-1292
202-223-2226
www.nof.org/prevention/ calcium.htm

Learn how you can boost your calcium intake by adding nonfat powdered dry milk to homemade cookies and other foods. A single tablespoon of powdered milk provides 52 mg of calcium.

CALCIUMinfo.com
www.calciuminfo.com/ hometxt.htm

Click on "Kids Korner" to learn how strong bones really are and how they heal when they break or fracture.

Geology of Mammoth Cave
www.nps.gov/maca/ geology.htm

This site explains how calcium deposits formed the Mammoth Cave some 350 million years ago in what is today Kentucky. Containing more than 335 miles (539 km) of underground passages, Mammoth Cave is the longest cavern system in the world.

Cave Pearls
www.extremescience.com/ CavePearls.htm

Read how calcium in water droplets dripped from the ceilings of caves to form pearls in the puddles below.

Soft Water and Suds
www.scifun.chem.wisc.edu/ HOMEEXPTS/SOFTWATR. html

Carry out an experiment to see how liquid dishwashing detergent acts in hard water.

Important Words

compound substance formed from the combination of two or more different elements

conductor substance through which electricity or heat passes

element building block of matter

enamel hard, protective layer that surrounds a tooth

hard water water that contains too much calcium and certain other substances

limestone rock formed from calcium carbonate shells that have been under pressure for millions of years

marble rock formed from limestone

matter stuff or material that makes up everything in the universe

osteoporosis bone disease caused by a lack of calcium

Index

Meet the Author

Salvatore Tocci is a science writer who lives in East Hampton, New York, with his wife Patti. He was a high school biology and chemistry teacher for almost thirty years. His books include a high school chemistry textbook and an elementary school book series that encourages students to perform experiments to learn about science. He had a water softener installed in his home to reduce the calcium level in his well water.

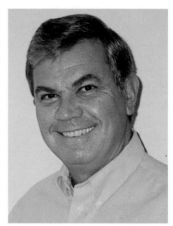